Behind These Fences

Behind These Fences

Poems by E. L.

Cover Art by Yusef Qualls-El
Cover Design by Casey Chiappetta
Text Design by Charlotte Lopez-Jauffret

BleakHouse Publishing
2020

BleakHouse Publishing

Ward Circle Building 254
American University
Washington, DC 20016

NEC Box 67
New England College
Henniker, New Hampshire 03242

www.BleakHousePublishing.com

Robert Johnson – Editor & Publisher
Charlotte Lopez-Jauffret – Chief Operating Officer

Copyright © 2020 by Robert Johnson

All rights reserved. No part of this book shall be reproduced or transmitted in any form or by any means, electronic, mechanical, magnetic, photographic including photocopying, recording or by any information storage and retrieval system, without prior written permission of the publisher. No patent liability is assumed with respect to the use of the information contained herein. Although every precaution has been taken in the preparation of this book, the publisher and author assume no responsibility for errors or omissions. Neither is any liability assumed for damages resulting from the use of the information contained herein.

ISBN-978-0-9961162-5-1-9000

Printed in the United States of America

Dedication

Dedicated to my progeny Datwon, Kemauri, Elijah Jr., Cara, Moses, and the daughter I never knew. A day doesn't go by without you all on my mind and I will never give up.

Table of Contents

Acknowledgements
Introduction

I
Language Undefined – 3
The Ritual -- 4
Behind these Fences – 5
After Sunset – 6
Time – 7
Incarnation – 8
I fix things – 9
Addiction – 10
I am – 11
Special Needs Health Care – 12
Drowning Child – 13
Beyond Fantasy – 14
Where am I now?– 15
Turtle – 16
Black Boy – 17
Changes – 18
Did I die? – 19
Strings – 20
Beautifully Blues – 21
Why do I think about a God – 22
Seeking Love – 23
I have something I want to say – 24
I want to be sorry – 25
Desperate – 26

II
Inner Wall – 30
Man Bird – 31
Rock Bottom – 32
Letter to the AW – 33
At least – 34
Afraid – 35
Our moments – 36
Ninja – 37
The Player - 38
Little Ninja – 39
Without rules – 40
A Teachers End – 41
Discovery after 4 years in Prison – 42

You Left Me – 43
Until we meet – 44
So the dirt asked the grass - 45
Now what – 46
An idiot cleaning - 47
Made Famous – 48
Begin and End - 49
Free time – 50
Moon Man - 51
Young Love - 52
Encourage potential - 53
Freedom - 54
When the beat ends - 55
Live - 56
Emotional strength - 57
Love? - 58
Life - 59
The Agnotologist – 60
I don't mean to be Short – 61
Elijah – 62
The series – 63
The Woman - 64
PR - 65
Everyday - 66
3am - 67
My Gift - 68
Bringing Back Belief - 69
Hello Summer – 70
What do you people do – 71
It's what I do I feel - 72
So what - 73
In the mirror - 74
Is it possible - 75

About the Poet – 76
About the Artists & Designers – 77
Other Titles from BleakHouse Publishing – 78

Acknowledgments

First and foremost, thank you Allah for your grace, mercy, and beautiful word, that continually inspires me to strive for greatness. Lord you have been the most important aspect of my life and your word has always kept me grounded without fear nor doubt. Thank you to my mother, aunt Maxine Bailey, and family who supported me when everyone else seemingly forgot. Father I am so grateful for the creative talents you so humbly passed down to me, you've always encouraged and supported me even when your love seemed more tough than loving.

To the volunteers of the ID13 project, Halle Neiderman for being me muse in the beginning, and pushing our group as a whole to topics outside the confines of the prison walls, you were an absolute joy to be around. Special thanks to Christopher Dum, without you this wouldn't be possible. You truly made me believe in humanity again, you accepted a bunch of strange misunderstood individuals in your life and helped us find our voices. You've taken a chance believing in me, when I had long given up on myself. To Hilary, Bengt, Sony, and Theodore Poland, you took on this responsibility going above and beyond your call of duty.

To James Bigley from the Cleveland Magazine, for expanding our exposure to the public. You captured us as we were, men with something to say, not just hardened criminals. Your article was poetic and your words sang across the pages. To Donyale Robinson for lightening the mood, keeping the peace and helping me relax during down time. Jarrett Southerland for listening to some of my works and at times helping me to capture the true essence of my aesthetic prose. To my Pumpkin Rose it's better to have known love, then to have never loved at all. You challenge me and made every day worth it.

To the publisher your vision and skills made this book work.

I want to give an extra special thanks to all my brothers in faith. Sami Ayoub for constantly teaching and guiding me with the Lords words, and never losing focus, Rickey Alexander you been my voice of reason, and most critical critic. You lead me out of the days of the wall, helped me to think logically when I got emotionally carried away, and kept me on the proper echelon. Benjamin Nunley your one of the smartest brothers I know and you always answer my questions even though I always have to tell you to dumb down your responses. Kenneth Hopkins you were a role model in patience and knowledge, your positive influence on everyone around you was uncanny. I hope one day I could also lead by your example. Anibel Santiago even though you hated me in the beggining we've grown extremely close. To Ronzel Haynesworth, William Stevens, Naquel Gadson, Leontae Jones, and my loyal friend Troy Jones. You've been here for me, keep me in shape, and never ceased to lift my spirits, they say you never know you maybe entertaining angels unaware, may the Lord cover you in all you do my friend.

Last but certainly not least to all my readers, my goal was to connect with you all, spreading love, peace, and understanding, as we relate to one another. I hope we all meet one day in a place called freedom, with love Peace.

Introduction

Fences exist in many forms. In the American Dream, they are white picket. For E.L., his are tall and topped with razor wire. However, regardless of their form, fences serve to separate. They cordon off space and dictate where we can and cannot be. In some cases, they are built in ways that dictate what we can and cannot see. Fences never speak to us. They never urge us toward empathy or bring us closer. Fortunately, there is a gift that we all possess that enables us to reach through any barrier and connect with one another. We have our words.

In this collection, E.L. reminds us that no matter who we are, or where we are, our words have the power to lay claim to our experiences as human beings. I first met E.L. in the summer of 2016 when I began volunteering at Lake Erie Correctional Institution in Northeast Ohio. While our lives differ in many ways, his writing consistently reminds me of the universal truths that we all face. E.L.'s pieces speak to us through love, hurt, hopes and dreams, and a search for truth and meaning. Let them speak to you and your life. Let them speak to your world, to E.L.'s world. Let them speak to our world.

Christopher Dum | ID13 Prison Literacy Project | www.id13project.com

PART I

Language Undefined

How we define language if not by expression
Like the government pleases the rich to keep us from a depression
To the musicians it's keeping tune in rhythm with percussion
And to me it's my poetic writings and influential discussions
Oh how religious continually focus on connections
And how the painters brush strokes flow into our paintings
Or how the dreamer dreams all we can imagine
If only our language is communicated by expression
The lover shoes love with feelings and in actions
And surely the cunning linguist like the twist in their passions
The swimmer swims the fighter fights and eternal is everlasting
But what is language when it's thrown and there is no one catching?
Is expression an expression if there no one watching?
Like this and that are professionals from the noun that their suggesting.
So what do you call aimless talk and words beyond our understanding
If language is spoken and written for human communication

The Ritual

Ritual oh ritual teach me something spiritual. Light from my eyes only give me something visual. Blood thru my veins so I'm feeling something physical. Power of the TV always showing something sexual. Ritual oh ritual I'm looking for the spiritual life after death so this time is only miniscule. I'm trying to understand so this realm is very questionable. Wonder whom I'm seeing in my sleep is unexplainable. Ritual oh ritual searching for the spiritual. Truth is in some books but some books are not reasonable. Trying to find the reason but the Preachers are not reliable. Asking why Lord but our Lord is not responsible. Ritual oh Ritual I'm missing something spiritual want to see God but the face is unimaginable. Guided by the Love of the Living Most Merciful. Heaven on Earth can this statement be obtainable. Ritual oh ritual give me something spiritual. I'm praying and I'm praying and I'm praying for what I'm praying for. Praying for a miracle praying is the ritual. Pray til something happen then believe it's only magical. Ritual oh ritual show me something spiritual. I'm confessing that the blessing in your lessons are so beautiful. No stressing in your testing while I'm seeking the unusual. Questing towards the essences of the natural metaphysical. Ritual oh ritual created by the spiritual. Created by the ritual oh spiritual oh spiritual far beyond the Ritual.

Behind these Fences

Woe to these fences caging us we raging let us free.
Personalities crash and theories collide
masculinity gets confused with ego and pride.
Check ins crash outs and fake suicide
I'm not Maya Angelou but still I rise but still I rise.
Look into these eyes there is no we in this team
just so many I's why can't we have a dream
Behind these fences
Our thoughts get like the thickest fog unable to see mountains
Actions flow like waters subconscious orders
make the heart beat faster sorta
like a computer without a user knowledgeable hoarder
Brain teaser crowd pleaser can we cross the border
Black Islamic immigrants or terrorist for ya
Death to the infidels not Isis that's American lawyers
Behind these fences
When it comes to minorities they legalized slavery
Slavery is existent for all of us within
We are dead and dying slaves seeking freedom once again.
Who will make amends for the 13th amend
I've done a crime so my life is not mine beginning to end
lock down in our lock down these gates designed only to let us in
The Hole programing us to fear but need segregation like original sin
Behind these fences
sleep counted eat play counted eat sleep repeat
a bunk and a number become a tomb and a tombstone
What was made to be temporary has become our permanent home
Behind these fences.

After Sunset

Seeking the pureness and promise of the lights mercy
We're good for now in this terrible cycle of normality
cursed with life's shortness dammed is the penalty
Bleak is the common and death is the certainty.
happiness is scarce mostly sadness and poverty
No gain without pain so there's no gain with serenity
peace is a fairytale and war is reality
Shock troop Devil dogs hear comes the cavalry
Many are with illness ignorance and disability
Fabricated foods filled with poison feeds humanity
Production moves widely mass marketing our glutany
Still racism and prejudice is the modern day slavery.
Thinking in the Dark speaking blind to the cowardly.
Even Lucifer does want God wills what's righteousness to the Godly
So who are we to ignore the laws then believe we are holy?
In our dark selfish hell we are lost and we are Lonely.
After sunset when our thoughts run wildly.

Time

Invisibly visual seen beyond all things, in all things,
operating like a father disciplining and protecting all things.
Healing and decaying without end,
An unseen beginning numbering the days within
your perfect judgment calculated and precise. Absolute and definite certain while sleepless in your continuous work you never exhaust how do you even exist.
Can anything exist without you if you are father where is mother?
Is she Earth or is she Nature where's the kids or is this a tale of old wives
Are you the same in all the other planets stars and lives.
Seeking answers without reason is it you that change the seasons?
In death we will surely know you watching us watch you let us go.
With Time.

Incarnation

When I vision institutional life what do I see? Where someone from the outside looking in would see murderers, rapist, alcoholics, thieves, drug users, drug abusers, drug dealers, evil doers aka villains like Dr evil, the enemy, or as the Godly would call us "sinners". Thrown behind fences, walls and cages like savage beast or mistreated pets to keep others unlike us safe from us. What I see, although some act or call themselves savage, I see a group of my peers. Some young some old all different races and nationalities. Fathers, sons, brothers, uncles, grandfathers, and nephews all different but the same. I see men who took what life offered them and made choices to get thru to the next day some choices made just to make it through the next minuet but we made these choices and we own it. We are the men who see life from all aspects we can taste both good and bad we have seen ugly and vile. We know what it takes to do what you have to do without excuses. Whether or not our choices were misleading, misguided, rash, indecisive, or just plain ignorant we learn and adapt. Not all of us get it, some get worse and continue to be lost and confused but before your freedom begins to make judgements.
What if you were innocent just living your judgmental life and suddenly your freedom was taken away? Could your bodies handle the improper bedding, the hard water, the below average food, the mental stress, or the reality of seeing and hearing about deaths from suicide and lack of proper health care. How about the strain it puts on the family, parents and children. Would your judgmental freedom be there to help you rise above this "Just Us System" and truly bring some justice if this position was yours? We are the future, believe that incarceration is like a womb preparing us for life like it was something new. We are molded into model citizens prepared to be positive and productive. Most prison stories aren't positive but if you believe in change then we together can be the difference.

I fix things

I break and repair to take and remake to make anew
something that was once old.
Like two sweaters into one hoody two pockets with one sting
pulled tight to keep light warm in the dark cold
I fix things.
Wired to electronic pulses to wire to grounded faucets only
to avoid electronic faults
It's like electronics talks to me... through you God.
I fix things.
unbroken no need to enhance
like factory to after market to change the stance
just for a glance

where is your satisfaction in your creation
always sad never happy always changing
just to please my selfish devotion
to worldly looks appearance's and the crooks lust.
I fix things its a must.
My father planted his seed to make a tree
than you banzaied me
dwarfed me in your little pot twisted my arms with wires
fashioned me to your choices then sent mockers to heckle
your disfigurement
mental stressing punishment
all to your amusement then give me the ability to fix things
unseen stranger with your whispering menace I'm still living
so you're not finished the testing.
the struggle before the blessing
the storm before the calming
the trail by fire the same with gold purifying and other
precious metals.
I fix things.
like the rain for a draught or a friend to the lonely
Striving for contact from the only
source without strife.
My Lord what happen to my life?
I fix things.
still some repairs I cannot see
I'm broken yet I cannot fix me.

Addiction

The lack of ability, the absence of being able for a specific purpose according to the social norm. Handicapped or abnormally formed. Special. Weird. Helpless and or useless. Depression, anxiety, mentally anguish, all because I can't reach the limitless heights because my lack of feet if only I could step over these fences. This prison is only a disability to non-Giants and folks that fear pain and punishment. Would climbing through razor wire excite the one who likes to cut themselves or segregation torment for the introvert? Disability is only a Judgement in the eye of the judgmental. I'm fully disabled but the unknown is what I've known not to be able to do. Here is a your ability Dis: I can do anything you can do better, I can do anything better than you.

I am

I am your reality blocker, your internal pessimist. I ensure whatever you decide goes wrong. I keep the finger pointed at you. Because we both know you suck. I am not a whisper. I am loud and continuous voices. What is a good day when you're not okay. I devour happy thoughts and drain all positive energy from my house and all those around. I am more than just a thought. Beyond an emotion I affect to the bone and all your action. I am very able, not a disability. It's not me, it's you. I'm king. I am depression.

Special needs health care

It effects all people within the institution an inmate has a disabling injury prior to incarceration and because the lack of care staff find themselves in arguments losing jobs due to law suits money lost.
Please I'm asking for all hands on deck there are fellow inmates falling left and right. Wheel chairs with no wheels Guys with one eye no eye patch guys with broken arms no arm sling people with nubs and no proper nub lube. The time is now we can't keep allowing these people to overlook the lube less nub having eye less without patches. We must take a stand for those who can't stand and take a knee for those without knees. Open your ears for the deaf speak up for the dumb. Don't just sit we must be hands on for the nubs. So let us be handy for the handicapped. All jokes aside Core Civic doesn't care about inmate injuries.

Drowning Child

As the living water swallows the whole of us slowly pulling us into its belly. We search for our voice but can only find the lack of air and panic. What a test we've got ourselves into. Why would we dive in? Quickly we seek our options as desperation settles, looking up into the light and our father's hand. What is this life? so many beautiful currents pulling and twisting us this way and that, filling every moment with a brilliance unfathomable to the spectrum of our consciousness. At this moment only in the struggle is it clear. We can see the light and our fathers hand within it, a clear path where only shallow water and small bubbles like parables block our reach but we fear his worried grasp and the salvation from our dire state, instead we search in the far distance something new and uncertain. We learn a new thing floating away from the familiar,
and in it we reach our motionless fate
lost in a strange and unnatural state
disconnected from what once gave us breath.
Death

Beyond Fantasy

Can you see me in these words in the sounds of the airs as it ushers the oxygen combined with h2 in all solids and liquids?
Can you see me through the windows to my soul the ocular cavities that presents its messages to the lightless void between my ears?
Can you see these thoughts the vision of completion that is but isn't only my mentality?
Can you see beyond the vast layers of mask that covers the beauties that is the natural form of me?
Can you see the dancing rays playing with the darkness the red orbs orbiting my silhouette saturating the emptiness that is my caged reality?
Can you see my challenges the reachless heights of my deformities my effortless efforts to just be?
Can you see the beings behind the voices that operate on my decisions like a doctors precision incisions blurring my good vision to do righteousness in this surgery of my life path?
Can you see me spearheading the separation of science and math the maniacal unachievable fact in this statement because clearly there is a division like light and time?
Do you have vision to see beyond the negative presumptions created by your own personal reflections and prejudmental prejudice. Do you see I am you and everyone else is me?
Can you see our similarities?
Can you see that when the power of love overcomes the love of power that we can find peace?
I was born Elijah before I became human but can you see? Noticing that they kill the positive people and let the demons run free?
What is the evil eye without the images you repeatedly show clearly?
Open your mind and ...See beyond the fantasy.

Where am I now?

I'm in a mental penitentiary inside this walls are closing in on me
I'm waiting for the day that I can open up these doors that block the path in front of me.
My mind is blank no normal imagery like blurry lines that's lacking symmetry.
Unfocused thoughts of drugs and alcohol and sex in prison what has gotten into me.
Was freed to be tricked into slavery, out cast separate from society. metaphorical tragic death taken me from the true love ones that I called my family.
How can they hold me if I'm g.o.d. mistreating me like I'm d.o.g. The injustice system makes our civil rights invisible under this G.O.V.
Go to school to get trapped into slavery higher learning for debts and poverty
Cause your status is classified by your amount of money and your amount of property. How can this be what are they teaching me We're still slaves they said that was history. The rich stay rich and the poor stay poor You got to be kidding me.
SPIN

Turtle

One day we received a gift it was such a wonderful thing
A small little turtle in a bucket of water
Our family was overwhelmed with gratitude and we wanted the turtle to feel the same..
We decided to clean an aquarium fill it with natural rocks, plants and, small feeder fish, then placed it within.
We purchased turtle pellets from the local pet store and everyday we watched our turtle friend.
We thought this aquarium was an upgrade from the bucket but there was a sadness that you could feel and see.
So after some time we released the turtle from its glass prison to a local pond it looked back at our family as to say thank you and we never seen it again.

Black Boy

We see you with your nappy hair
Soup cooler lips and big nose breathing air
America loves your style so great for entertainment
Especially when your blood spills over the pavement
We know we need you but you are not an equal
We need you like a mouse feeds an eagle
just a part of our eco system
Who cares about your dancing and African rhythm
We would be better off with you just working for free.
Oh we did that with slavery.

Changes

My favorite season is spring because of the delicate changes the Earth was designed to bring. The cold temperatures slowly fade the icy snow melts and the perennials begin to sprout in there splender. There is nothing more beautiful than rain fertilizing the fertile grounds like the males fulfilment to a mother's womb. The Earth is nothing more than an Egg awaiting growth the soil like a shell cracking only to let the leaves feed the yolk. Changes is nothing more than stages off life. When I was a boy I dreamed of my wife, and I always wanted kids. 6 was never enough but I achieved that dream. Now it all has changed just like the sprout I broke the soil grew to my predestined height bloomed my flower then withered away into this winter. Prison life is just like winter but just like the perennial I will wait until I can spring loose and yet again strengthen my roots. What a funny thing change is. Because my dream never changes. but does that make me insane because I dream of the same thing and expect a different result. Then be shocked when it's all brought to a halt. I rise up I fall I walk and I crawl from knelling to standing tall to once again laying beneath the soil. Yet love stays the focal point through it all from a poor man to the royal in that never Changing life cycle and its stages that never changes.

Did I die?

I no longer hear your voices and I haven't seen your faces since that day
my eyes closed and I arouse in a daze
I live in a endless repeat of the moments of my past
my constant is like one big flash
Back with silence from what I thought was love
This reality doesn't fit me like OJ's glove.
Up until now my emotions have been clear
Where am I and how did I get here?
Trapped behind fences charged by wires
Misery surrounds me and never tires.
Did I die and am I in heaven or hell?
and did these strangers around me die as well?
Free shelter, free food, and no more bills
Its too good to be true kinda gives me the chills
Where are all the people that I once known
and why these other people still using pay phones
Did I travel in time and cross some dimensional plane
So much has changed and it all seems so strange.
I can't hardly remember who I was before.
I'm so confused why are the locks on the outside of the door?
Where do they take those people after they get into a fight?
Some guy said "to the hole" now that doesn't seem right.
Does he mean to the grave for some sort of second death?
This dream sure is weird and one big mess.

Strings

We put strings on our acquaintances then call them friends
stinging them along like puppets.
Tightening the rope as they grow nevering wanting the real.
We want puppets that feel how we feel,
love what we love,
agree with every decision,
move like us and listen.
Not like us but for us more like by us,
to buy our affection by doing exactly what we want.
Puppeteers to the masses to be puppets for the masses

Beautifully Blues

Brown, green, clear, blue, and all the grays between.
Sweet smelling rain, crisp, and clean air.
Frolicking there amongst us, with invisible smiles.
For infinite miles, endless peace in the breeze.
Brilliant vibrant hues shades of blue, water dripping from
the trees
Happy little bush covering the lawn, surrounding a pond.
Just tadpoles within a stream, mammals and amphibians
fond, of the neurotic aquatic blue living thing.
Light made your colors bright, so beautifully displayed
Amazing spectrum sprayed, glowing geyser misting
wet sand glistening, listening to your natural jazz.
Dressed beautifully in blue, clear, green, and brown beneath
the grass
embedded deep converged in peace.
Soaked back into the grounds river motif.

Why do I think about God?

Is there any other way to believe?
Is there any other way to perceive?
To achieve the thoughts that we receive?
Peace love or need to confirm
not deceive for ease to please g.o.v's
To them its just a string
but to we its many things
maybe the most important and valuable
when we're reminded who we got it from
The amazing string a fire that always burns
burn them in ashes to fill our ERNs
smokeless flame kindled by men
judged by our king defined by sin
Man the fruit of God's creation.
Our lives this contemplation.

Seeking Love

Day to day seeking a way to never lose this joy. Like a sunny day cooled with gentle breeze and shady trees. The pollen count is low the scent from the flowers are high and the water is as blue as the sky. Like the smell of a baking cake from an open window and fresh sun kissed lemonade fills your glass laying there peacefully, towel laid upon the grass. Love is like every holiday when everything goes right and when the stars come out on clear moon lit night. Holding hands with the warms crystal sands of a lake side beach. Listening to the birds chirp as the water messages your feet love is the heartbeat that connects this world like the laughter of little boys and girls. innocent like a flower petal innocent and free love is everything and nothing to see sleeping close to the campfire deep scent of the wild pine smooth like babies milk thick like the eggs yolk charismatic and theatric yet simple in every way. love isn't something you feel alone it overwhelms all your senses because love is the experience.

I have something I want to say

How do the blind see the world
Negatively caused by harsh visual effects?
Zen with no sense of griefs
or blinded by opinions and judgements
How do the blind see the world
Can the blind lead a riot
or be the root to a bias thought based on visual difference
does the blind hate the way people look
or hate when people don't look like them
How do the blind see the world
Do they laugh when they see you fall
Curse when you make mistakes
or Stereotype your race
If everyone sound the same men like men and girls like girls
How do the blind see the world
Is everyday like a dream and every month the same
And except the temperature change
would anything look strange
If the blind could see the world.

I want to be sorry

I want to be sorry for my past
Sorry for my desires to make money fast
Sorry for the broken hearts and my fast ways
Sorry for my ignorance and them selfish days.
Sorry I didn't give love when I had the chance.
Sorry I didn't make more joyful days to dance
Sorry there is so many you's and only one me
Sorry it took so much time for me to see
Sorry for the many nights I left you alone
Sorry for never reaching out when I had access to a phone
Sorry to the world cause I never really cared
Sorry for the wasted days that we could've shared
Sorry I apologized to only repeat the same action
Sorry that being available wasn't my greatest addiction.
Sorry that these sorry words are just my sorry rant
Cause I can't be sorry for the things that molded me into a man.

Desperate

I'm desperate for attention
desperate for solace
desperate for love
desperate to be free
desperate to have knowledge
desperate for ignorance
I'm desperate to be strong
While I'm desperately weak
There is nothing more pure than the most sincere need
so I'm desperate to be desperate
desperate to be me.

PART II

Inner Wall

My Children are growing up and I stare so dreary at the wall.
Listening to my sad song
woe is me.
If I could only give up my life for a chance to spend with my wife the one I let get away
the one that I pushed away
the moments I lost. My descendants so small
oh wall
do you hear my plea for love.
My love for love of family and friendly encounters.
my tear drops have tear drops so deep my sadden state.
I miss even the quite times when you were all asleep
and now it's just me.
Wall are you listening
ignoring or echoing ?
I never moved my lips so I know it cannot be
sounds never break free I just stare at you
eyes welled up with deep thought of joys from the past
leaving me lonely and sad
lip poked out dragging along
singing my sad song
Woe as me.

Man Bird

I I was a bird in a cage
A snake came
I became a man
I felt the fear as the bird
And the strength as the man
As a protector I reached in my hand
grabbing the snake by its throat
Setting the bird free. but endangering me.
The man was still bit.

Rock Bottom

I rode my rusty off brand bike along
The unmaintained back road of the
Ghetto I called my neighborhood.
Trees overgrown choking the path
As I choked on the joint I smoked
To ease the truth that life would never
Be much more than this. My chain
Popped from my pos of a bike
And I fell quickly to the pavement
Here lies death to fall right next
To a dead body thrown amongst the
Overgrown bush. This must be rock
Bottom.
My father screams for me to let
The dog out I knew he hated the
Dog I knew my puppy was meaningless
To him. Nothing like fresh
Roadkill the truck came out of
Nowhere and my puppy bled out
This must be rock bottom.
My grandma died and so did my
Family my mother is now a single
Parent Divorce must be rock bottom
I tried to skip a rock once I think it hit
Rock bottom

Letter to the AW

I quit
I woke up one day and decided enough was enough
I need to go
This isn't my job nor my choice career
So tell the boss I will not be here
Not for any of his closed meetings
The Managements inappropriate greetings
His crazy daily lock downs
no more employee chow lines
blue uniforms or walless cubicals
the process foods in a predesignated box
in a predesignated space with a combination lock
This isn't the job for me.
So tell the boss I want to leave.

At least

I'm may not be tall but at least I reach for the soaring heights
I may be nowhere now but at least I have a goal in sight
I may be weird but at least I'm a brilliant
I may move too fast but at least I'm not a procrastinator
I may not be happy but at least I smile
My hair may be nappy but at least I have style
I'm in a prison but I know it's just a phase
A long bumpy road filled with sad and lonely days
but at least I have my faith.

Afraid

Seeking to be apart of the oh so natural urge
An urge to merge with beautiful words
Words like a woman with her natural curves
Soft sensual with a natural girth.
moist like the waters in our mother Earth
A mother with wombs for natural birth.
I am but a man with the natural urge
An urge to merge with beautiful words
Struggle to own up to his worth.

Our moments

Accented
By events
Created in this
Dunya
Eager to
Fall in love
Genuinely and
Honestly
Insanely searching for
Joy just another foolish
Kook
Looking for family lusting for fantasy only for
Moments in time
Nothing last forever but
Our moments. Our moments are
Perfection and perfection is perceivable together. A
Quantum complete and whole. My beliefs are
Radical in this
Simulation of sincere sentiment.
Together
Universally connected through
Volumes of laws
Warranted for each second of this
Xenology
Yes interrelationships I'm stuck A
Zealot for loving our moments.

Ninja

I wanted to be a ninja
but I'm too emotional
so attached to my victims
Attached to my gear
Attached to the sharpness of my blade
If my emotions would just fade
I would hide in the shade
Deep in the shadow
I wouldn't feel so hollow
I would finally have purpose
A ninja hired for service
Never tired never worried
Always masked Always blurry
quick and slick stars thrown in fury
knives and darts blown
but this fault is my own
internal commotion stuck in Emotion
A ninja

The Player

I had saxophones
The order from recorder
playing saxophones
one after another note after note
let the saxophonist blow
marching behind the drummers beat
seated in the jazz bands seat
First chair oh yeah I was good
I had saxophones.

Little Ninja

I was called a ninja
but why I don't recall
I was young and small
playing ball with friends
and the ball struck the lense
of a tall pink man's car
his faced turned red
and that's when he said
I hate you little ninjas.

Without rules

without rules I would shut down
rules I would fade away
rules I would bend time and
rules to change space.
confined in this body with these rules that I must face
without rules I would rule and choose my own fate.
No caps on my money
no caps on my health
no caps on my living
no caps on my wealth
if these rules could be broken no nudes prohibited
no news would be sad and the blues would have new meaning.
What wisdom would we live in where rules was not bound
would light still be faster than sight and all sound.
Bass like the beating heart
faith like you crying out
rules couldn't hold you back
death would not be found
war would be over
scream peace with a final shout
without rules to rule I would refuse to stay down.
Fly

A Teachers End

In contemplation of my life completion
Knowing what I ought be teaching
A lesson aimed for those to remember
Like the fated cold that comes with winter
A thirst for warmth in those frigid months
A lesson learned from tragic stunz
A teaching a preaching a pastor's voice
Oh how I pondered on my chilling choice
what once seemed easy has destine came
to clear me from my in prisoned brain
depression pain and defeating grief
A noisy wrenching like gritting teeth
In chalk I write my frozen frame
Outlined to mark the chilling scene
A teachers heart without a beat
ended and cold along the street.

Discovery after 4 years in Prison

My anxiety is real
These guys can see
I'm not real too tall
But tall's not real to me
My anxiety is overwhelming
I just want released
These guys are like animals
Caged until released
Sweating beneath the weights
My anxiety is my prison
Inside here I am free
My writing is investigative
Investigative and wild like the ruminants
Like the majority of these guys wild
Men acting as a child
After 4 years nothing has
Changed for the overseers
Spin moves are surely the same

You Left me

For a moment we are together
Time like a breath in the blinking of an eye
Like a shooting star tear fall...
How small our time together
We Now so far apart.
Each beat from my internal drum
Like a lightning strike of memories of joy
Pulled between the two then and now my lonely present.
Woe to our past we lived such happy days
Peace now brings so much pain.
I rather the white noise of chaos to drown the darkness of the serene.
You left me and yet you took me with you
Hanging there from the supporting beam.
My life a nightmare and no relief in my dreams.
We were perfectly together but you didn't hear my internal cry.
So I tied the noose kicked the chair and said
Goodbye.

Until we meet

I haven't met you yet, but I assure you something
You appreciate what you have when you have nothing
When we want for nothing
Yeah we just be frontin'
Ain't nothing like a woman when you need some loving
So here's the facts and truth
Yeah I'm feeling you
I know you need love and I need it too
Yeah I'm locked up but my hearts free
My emotion and devotion give you all of me
like a fantasy I'll fulfill ya dreams
and until we touch its by any means
Let me ease your mind I won't let you go
Why complicate what is pure and natural
We should be together we could find Love
Every storm weathered would define us
let's just be happy and together we
Be forever us when we finally meet.

So the dirt asked the grass

When was the last time you lived amongst the tree's
made a path through the leaves
or lay in the flower bed with the bees
Watching As they pollinate life for those honey thieves
Felt death and demise lay to nourish the earth
as the worm helps the rotting flesh turn to dirt
The rain spray to show its worth
and the seed sprouts such a marvelous birth.
When was the last time you've enjoyed such splendor
examining each snowflake in the white of December
As the hues of blue change hear the ice whimper
feel the chilling and cold burn of an icicle splinter.
Have you ever shook violently when your face screamed burr
Waiting patiently for the weather change at the end of the winter
turning brown then green or hot red with a temper

Now what

Man found on highway getting high but when asked to pull over
The car sped up
Self-driving cars don't care about flashing lights

A idiot cleaning

I'm such an idiot
why do I keep all this junk
An old magazine with one picture of some girl I will never meet
These holy socks also old
am I hoarding?
Wall I know you hear my talking to you
looking silly with those gnats and that tape I stuck on you just in case
Just in case of what exactly I don't know? Speaking of cases I now have three or two cases for things I am pretty sure I don't need.
But look at all my shit
three watches three pairs a shoes one pair of Boots and
Pants so many pants and I only wear the one.
Towels and sheets and shirts folded neat bracelets and bands and wait
what is this on my stand a pass from 2 months ago.
I'm sure it's time to let that go I know I got bags and plenty of rags and bowls
hats and a necktie
now why do I have that?
Can't forget my belts and shorts of all sorts some for show some for sport
and some I never wear but its mine so I don't care.
Spring cleaning is for fools and I'm an idiot so I will keep it all.
OK wall let's compromise you keep your tape but remove the gnats and I guess
I can delete so of my old messages from the Jpay.

Made Famous

Made famous like a leaked sex tape yes
The day decided I will never see my family again.
Forever empty like a vacant metaphorical residence.
A address that never receives mail, from the beginning and ending moons.
A fool too pitiful to deserve a laugh or empathy.
Thus am I, but a casted humanoid shadow, where light will never shine.
The speck where not even the fly would land or its maggot form.
The unsightly, the mocked then forgotten.
The one who has cowered in fear of self and surrendered in shame.
Adducted by the affliction of addiction.

Begin and End

Whenever life ends and death begins
Begins like living free
Free from the life in which follow
Follow to some Aha moments
Moments that will end our life
Life, the greatest show on Earth
Earth in which we aim to please
Please others from the top.
Top like the highest level.
level like the echelon from which we fell.
Fell like a lightning strike.
Strike it rich.
Rich by freeing our mind.
Mind free from the death in peace.
Peace to be found whenever.

Free time

Our time is purchased for currencies in search of moments of Joy.
As we grow we lose those we loved, and once lusted for.
Ticking away, all is lost bought for such a miserable cost.
Many moments of happiness lost because...
As we grow we hope to gain the joy that went, with all our time spent.
Happiness has not a fee, since internal peace is free.
We still waste time and space just for the smiling face
when inwardly we hate the chase for happiness and joy.
Spent in the agony we earn, and all our energy burned with only one lesson learned. The guarantee Happiness is free... but time isn't.

Moon Man

I have tried my best to be a good man and I yet to have found a good woman.
Maybe it's me and I don't understand the complicity of their emotions.
I feel I'm logical and attempt to be optimal in my ways of love.
Maybe I'm too physical and forget to listen or maybe my hearing is selective.
I believe I can be corrected but somehow I'm not effected until I'm threatened.
And I still try to be a good man and I yet to have found a good woman
Maybe I couldn't cause maybe I shouldn't label them.
Am I only good or bad shades and the woman a light that never fades?
Or I a man only seeking to persuade a woman to shine on me.
As if I am the moon and she my sun.
Or am I the sun and she the reflecting one?
Surely I try to be a good man.

Young Love

When I was young I felt rhythmic poems with rhyming endings.
Defined romance casual flirting and sensual meetings.
I was a hopeless boy picking simply flowers
Eager for a date of holding hands for hours.
Spent the day at the mall and the night at the movies.
or a walk through the park when only love would move me

The people would stare cause they all would know
We showed the world our young love would grow.
A kiss on the cheek cuddled tight on the bleachers
Around giggling friends and flustered teachers

We didn't care for flaws 'cause we were oh too happy
Loving, campy, and oh so cheesy

Encourage potential

Do we honestly take the time to encourage ourselves.
Encouraging the things that we do well
moving with the sounds and flow of the world.
The world that continually strives to grow build and spread
Naturally seeking its source of strength
Light like the sparks that fires in you brain
From each thought big or little lights fires
Striking like a storm cloud full of knowledge
Wisdom, truth, fear, hate and Love
Do we honestly encourage this light?
Do we seek this light, this strength, this nourishment
that naturally makes us build and grow?
The light in our movements, and tasty sounds
Energy never fears pain nor can it be found crying
So we can surely leave this life without dying?

Freedom

Love Hate Next word
physics Side kicks
Hip thrust breast feet legs
Chicken moist center
Dinner
Cat Roars Lion Breath
Flaming bricks microphoned hits recorded
Sex sells.

When the beat ends

Blank thoughts happen in rhythm to take me to a place
where darkness meets light and creates a spark.
Actions control each action that react to that fact.
Without rhythmic thoughts my heartbeat doesn't stop.
Regardless of what I think it beats.
Till death brings the end of the death thoughts in life.
And thoughts can no longer continue.

Live

Living isn't just all hurt pain and struggle.
Even for a man in prison seemingly fighting the devil.
High negative energy where everyone is a possible enemy.
Inner bullies and downing judgments this isn't happy
being exactly where you supposed to be.
Would you ever want to sleep if you were living your dream?
Would you stop climbing if what you want was in reach?
Why guess if you already know the answer?
Procrastination and hesitation is just fear of failure.
Chase your goal and live.

Emotional strength

We should stretch our emotions like a yoga pose breathing.
Exercising our trust like a body builders muscle expelling
fear like the weakness it is. Conquering the pain of fear
knowing that it's the pain that brings the change of results.
Instead of being lazy lovers and emotional slubs.
Thus is challenge of emotional growth.
Peace is the goal of emotional strength.

Love?

What must I do to prove I'm capable of Love. Capable of loving deserving of the chance for sentiment.
Sentiment from a relationship of moral, indeed an oath isn't only oral.
I will put in the work yes I'm willing to work for what I desire. Let us let the qwerty keys be enough, as our words become bound to our hearts and the papers in which we said "I Do" for.
A covenant.
Yes I will do more cause our relationship should be ours and none should have claim over it.
Am I capable?
I've decided that questioning this fact confirms my incompetence.
Love is unmistakable from sight to feel but we still question is it real?

Life

This is my life
I smile when I am angry
I refuse to frown
This is my life
and it wont let me down
I found the beauty in the adornment
of that in which was made to be adorned.
surely beauty is beyond the vision of the eye
This is my life
My way my path
My choice to live without raft
to remain worry free
and laugh.
This is.
My
Life.

The Agnotologist

Why yes I speak in a domesticated state in fear.
My knowledge is limited to what I was taught
I don't ask no questions Sacred Cow
Surely my sentence I will sign in ignorance
because you have in favor my best interest
13 years no need to explain with my limited brain
Yes I know nothing I'm empty
Come now with your agnotology
Don't worry I'm not a actor
and my intelligence is not a factor
I do yes its true yes I am sheepish
Freakish even creepish I believe sex is love
but this is the norm I had to conform
My stupidity is attractive like clay and this is the way
My royalties is the royalty engraved in my DNA
So no matter your compulsion
I remain pious.

I don't mean to be Short

Nothing more fulfilling then stopping my day just to write and show I care.
As busy as I always am a few hours for you is just a droplet of time.
Time well spent, time well deserved, so much time it takes 'cause I take my time.
Something that could be done in minutes takes days
Something that should last for years could end
in seconds
So I take my time to write and then write once again
for the proof in my words
to ensure that those droplets are the truth and my words
Are at its most adequate and accurate Response.
Yes the Missive to the Miss's
Such droplets become ponds and from ponds to rivers that flow like the tears that will rage down my face from speaking in some way that I never truly meant.
All because the mood I was in.
Please forgive me for all those days of being Short.

Elijah

My styles is heartless these teenage years having started this the whole world holding me down like a hostage I finally lost it I need to end it so I can leave this flipped out world and stop getting splifted my mind stay lifted off this knowledge I hold off them days of being fake and trying to be bold trying to be cold trying to crack that hold of this bad present life that's trying unfold. and until my death I'm a try and decode that code that hold people stupid as they grow old walk the streets with they mind not open but closed basic instructions before leaving earth finally story to be told peep it evil always reenters the heart Earth I was told the key to life is knowledge but all eyes is closed drugs fights and money is the clip that we load cause your mind is a gun empty the clip and reload be a leader and don't you take that road behind bars in pain and now paying the toll. working hard in a cage just to get that blow like serving fiends like a plow when you push that snow. Still serving cane with a cane if you get that old. huh

The series

Love became anger and peace became a challenge
A birth became a death such is the series.
A fight became a makeup and sick became a cure
some bricks became a building and a hole became a door
such is the series
a theory became a fact and real became fiction
single became family and sober became addiction
Serious became silly and such is the series.
when a comedy becomes a romantic drama
a SciFi horror film becomes the series.

The Woman

Lord knows I love the woman if I only knew how to love the woman. Admiring all her curves and edges, desiring her natural allure.
Soft hands pampered nails, moist lips, and long lashes under arched brows, accenting her emerald like eyes.
Each of her hair follicles worth a touch, worth a taste, worth the count. Measure by measure scanning them all.
Her every breath worth a billion of my own, her heart like a song within a treasured chest, with spherical crowns worth a kiss.
Lord knows I love the woman if I only knew how to love the woman and cherish her like this.
There would be nothing I would miss I would sit and listen, attentive to her voice.
I would not ignore her choice.
She'd be mine and I'd be hers my time spent to serve... Her
It's so amazing a shining light like hers.
If I only learned to love the woman Lord knows I would love the woman because its love she deserves.

PR

Rose petals soft scented easily dented pumpkin shell hard to
smell inside tender smashed amongst a Halloween street
craved beaten bashed and eaten for a season
rose petals soft soft scented hand delivered
temporary gift for apologies and passion
Why must I dwell on her smell
the delicate pumpkin rose

Everyday

Everyday spent with you is like a day in Disney land and each moment is like a month on Mars because my heart soars through the stars. My feelings are hot and rich like vacation in Dubai its like taking trips to paradise when I look into your eyes. You are the happy moments of my tired soul..

3am

The day I get is full of things
But with you I stop just
To write
Such simple words are
Just enough to end lonely
Man's gripe
I seek your love I sought
Your touch but writing is
All I need
I end my day just for
You sometimes writing past
3...am

My Gift

365 days + 1 for the leap I took towards you.
I sit and stare into the distance admiring what could one day be within my touch.
The sparkling in your eye more spectacular than any star in the heavens, and experiencing your smile is like living an endless dream.
your lips and ears like sweet pieces of candy worthy of a gentle nibble.
Your hair like silk and your scent prepared for a taste.
I shall not waste even a nanosecond of the time we share. I'm stuck contemplating a love that should be done with sentimental precision, so I will make the best of it.
intimately and slowly taking care to notice each of our sensitive points of arousal. Ambitiously aiming only to please in the most of erotic desire, continually tapping your center repeatedly, for the moments of explosive overwhelment.
Making you aware the I love loving you because it feels so good.
Devoted to your happiness, my fantasy, my love, my gift.

Bringing Back Belief

Say! simplify a set of core values
concepts understandings and wisdom.
Experiences for convenience, for moments presented.
¿How do you live in your lampoon?
Study and find truth to save the youthful wonder, to achieve in what you believe in. Before the indoctrination of discouragement, they, you, and them call growing up into the realistic mind set. Sounds real pessimistic from the once imaginative optimistic ways of the immature. Stop frowning upon and stifling the splendor that is the creative mind, building negative barriers that stop the flow of positive growth. Your thoughts are energy, that produce words, that are heard in waves, so. Let us set the stage, groundbreaking our relief, removing the grief, and bringing back belief.

Hello Summer

How nice of you to bring back my winter relationship there must be love in the air after all that wonderful rain and pollen. You know I never really noticed how much I disliked the cold until you came with your intense heat. A heat that makes me want a little cold but nothing like the winter. Wait no I think that suffering in the heat is best and the barn swallows created a nest right above our recreation building and one of them died, when our ceiling fan in the dorm. Yes summer indirectly you caused this bird to die so your an accessory to crime. Is that why your doing time? Every year the same thing death by heat exhaustion, dehydration, or cancer by sun burn. Yeah summer your kinda the bad with the good but we all make mistakes. Did you think just because you allowed people to swim outdoors there wouldn't be any casualties? DROWNING! Your super arrogant you know with your stupid firework show that I couldn't personally see in prison. Yup I said it your holidays aren't exactly exciting. Nothing like that of the fall winter or the spring. What is Yard day anyway its laughable is what it is. Summer I believe you deserve this time more than me.

What do you people do

When I first arrived into the institution I ask a guy so where do I get a cell phone he said hey young blood there's no phones here that was the good old days. I'd be like good old days what the fuck is the good old days in prison.
He responded young blood back when new guys didn't ask questions.

It's what I do I feel

It all seems to real sometimes the fog the rain the endless pain
Mental of course.
But I know it's all but an illusion here to cause confusion of what truth really is.
What a dream really is what is what things want to be or appear in our own personal understandings.
Like the sky is red sometimes but we all know its blue even though that not true because reflections can be deceiving.
Or that sun which looks small because of the distance but we know that's not true because one of us get darker while the other get skin cancer
burning from the lack of SPF
or some shit the government created to force us to buy when they probably are the ones that made those fucking rays burn us in the first place, destroying the ozone layer by creating SPF. Stupid poor fuckers is what the rich call it
But I would look down on the world too if I wasn't trying to be the pious asshole self-righteous prick that they forced me to be by indoctrinating me in school telling me how to feel.
Good isn't dark and black isn't pure
be scared of the night cause it cold and wrong
run to the light cause its right and warm.
Skin that is.
I am a robot in a dream like the zombies seeking brains. Do they even do that cause some dance to the thriller woe to MJ's killer government drones
without circuits with proper software.
My voice screams I don't care but my programing makes me feel its what I do.

So what

I sure hate writers all of them and all those who like to read. The validaters of those who use words to create themes and schemes on parchment.
The law makers and their signatures truly who can win? What a conundrum we got online power trips created by readers and writers of programs for readers and writers to have showdowns of who can use words properly as if each thought was their own property but foolishly forgetting they signed an agreement that says now that they placed these words in a public forum online on line in a line of lines made by enumerated beings counted by a program that is programmed to program you to always return. What lesson can you learn from this writer's bliss? Surely the internet is word heaven if indeed the heaven we read in some book wrote by some being is in fact just as it was described. Can words even have a heaven?
Words have a way of changing things but we claim they don't hurt. More people die from mental stress then physical stressors so whomever made up this 'words don't hurt' nonsense lied just as most writers do so it's easy for me to hate them. But I'm lying now but most will believe it's true because its written in a book that only in history will it be proven to be what it actually is. A writer's thoughts.

In the mirror

In my reflection I see imperfections
a man striving for a dream
I see eyes and lips but I can't find handsome
Just a shell hiding depression.
I see failure and unachieved goals
and the loneliness of a battered soul
No matter what I think I see
I can't see me.
in the mirror.

Is it possible

When did the candle flame exhaust and the flower petals whither and brown.
What happen to the dinner, wine and the romantic sounds.
Do the slow jams no longer get played and has chivalry past
Am I before my time or is this just a thing of the past
Has woman become more manly or the man too fancy
Has love become the action or the feeling of being randy.
What is lust? what is trust? what happen to us
And the days when marriage meant to ashes and to dust
How do we renew what has died.
Lord knows I tried removing the pride

About the Poet

How can one man make an impact in the hearts of the future? E. L., who was born and raised in Baltimore MD, sought to use his words. Through his experiences in life's ups and downs from depression, love and loss, religion, and other influences such as incarceration, E. L. attempts to tell his story and touch the hearts of his readers. His dream is that one day, when he's gone and forgotten, his words might mend a broken spirit like his own.

About the Artists & Designers

CASEY CHIAPPETTA is a researcher who studies the civil legal system and access to justice. She received her MS from American University in Justice, Law & Criminology.

YUSEF QUALLS-EL is an artist affiliated with the Prison Creative Arts Project

CHARLOTTE LOPEZ-JAUFFRET is pursuing a doctoral degree in Justice, Law & Criminology from American University. She received her Master of Forensic Science with a concentration in Forensic Molecular Biology from the George Washington University. While obtaining her masters, Charlotte worked as a DNA technician at a private lab, and later worked as a Forensic Intelligence Analyst for a state forensic science laboratory. She is pursuing research at the intersection of criminal justice and forensic science. She obtained a B.S. in Biology in 2015.

Other Titles from BleakHouse Publishing

Pagan, John Corley

Silent, We Sit, Emily Dalgo

Black Bone, Alexa Marie Kelly

An Elegy for Old Terrors, Zoé Orfanos

Up the River, Chandra Bozelko

Distant Thunder, Charles Huckelbury

Enclosures: Reflections from the Prison Cell and the Hospital Bed, Shirin Karimi

A Zoo Near You, Robert Johnson et al.

Origami Heart: Poems by a Woman Doing Life, Erin George

Tales from the Purple Penguin, Charles Huckelbury

Burnt Offerings, Robert Johnson

www.ingramcontent.com/pod-product-compliance
Lightning Source LLC
Chambersburg PA
CBHW070438010526
44118CB00014B/2092